MAR 1 4 2006

S0-BOR-659

39114000

EMM

READING POWER

School Activities

Drama Club

Rae Emmer

The Rosen Publishing Group's
PowerKids Press™
New York

Published in 2002 by The Rosen Publishing Group, Inc.
29 East 21st Street, New York, NY 10010

Copyright © 2002 by The Rosen Publishing Group, Inc.

All rights reserved. No part of this book may be reproduced in any form without permission in writing from the publisher, except by a reviewer.

First Edition

Book Design: Christopher Logan

Photo Credits: Maura Boruchow

Emmer, Rae.
Drama club / by Rae Emmer
    p. cm. – (School activities)
Includes bibliographical references and index.
ISBN 0-8239-5968-6 (lib. bdg.)
1. Theater–Production and direction–Juvenile literature. [1.
Theater. 2. Schools.] I. Title. II. School activities (New York, N.Y.)
PN2053 .E46 2001
792'.0232–dc21

                                        00-013248

Manufactured in the United States of America

Contents

Putting on a Play   4

Getting Ready   6

Helping with Costumes   14

Taking a Bow   20

Glossary   22

Resources   23

Index   24

Word Count   24

Note   24

Putting on a Play

We are going to put on a play.

Getting Ready

The teacher helps us get ready.

Some of us are learning the words we will say.

Some of us are painting
stage props.

This boy helps with the lights.

Helping with Costumes

Parents help with costumes.

They help with makeup.

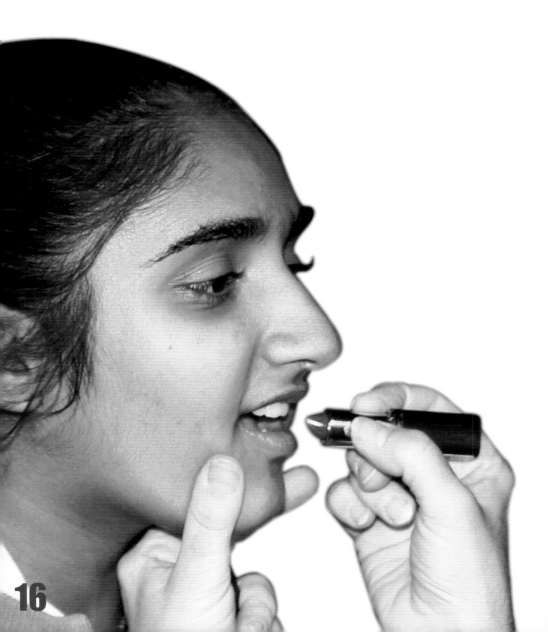

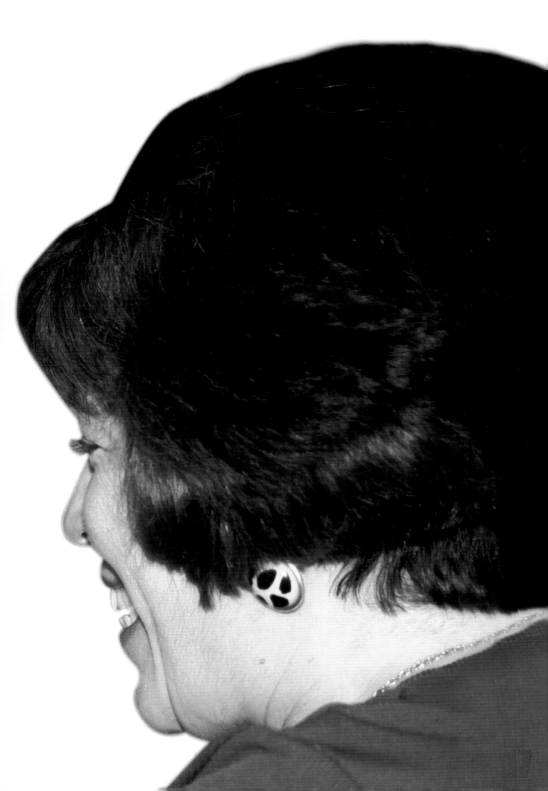

We do the play for
our families.

Taking a Bow

At the end of the play,
we bow.

Glossary

bow (**bow**) to bend at the waist

costumes (**kos**-toomz) clothes put on to look
like someone else

makeup (**mayk**-uhp) what is put on the face,
such as lipstick or powder

props (**prahps**) objects used by actors in a play

stage (**stayj**) a place to put on a play

Resources

Books

Putting on a Play: The Young Playwright's Guide to Scripting, Directing, and Performing
by Nancy Bentley and Donna Guthrie
Millbrook Press (1996)

Theater Magic: Behind the Scenes at a Children's Theater
by Cheryl Walsh Belville
Lerner Publishing Group (1986)

Web Site

Children's Creative Theater Guide
http://tqjunior.thinkquest.org/5291

Index

B
bow, 20

C
costumes, 14

L
lights, 12

M
makeup, 16

P
play, 4, 18, 20
props, 10

S
stage, 10

T
teacher, 6

Word Count: 60

Note to Librarians, Teachers, and Parents

If reading is a challenge, Reading Power is a solution! Reading Power is perfect for readers who want high-interest subject matter at an accessible reading level. These fact-filled, photo-illustrated books are designed for readers who want straightforward vocabulary, engaging topics, and a manageable reading experience. With clear picture/text correspondence, leveled Reading Power books put the reader in charge. Now readers have the power to get the information they want and the skills they need in a user-friendly format.